I've designed a notebook to keep journal of your reflections and be your companion on this journey.

You can buy it where you buy the book.

Pivotal Edge – Your New Career Perspective

ISBN: 978-91-990093-1-5

Edited by Henning Bech
Method testing with Julie Fornander & Tina Esbech
Test reading by Jillian Williams
Proofreading by B. Buddy
Cover and book design by Henning Bech
Published by Henning Bech AB (SE5594603994)

Dedication

To Elena, Katerina and Sofia

–the three most important people in my life-

without their unwavering support,

love and patience this book

would never have seen

the light of day.

In memory of

Karen Gertz and John Bech

My parents spent a lifetime writing,

playing with words and enjoying

the journeys reading books

took them on.

ACKNOWLEDGMENTS

Special thanks

To Julie and Tina.

Thank you for your feedback

and your patience with me

as we worked through

optimizing the models.

To Jillian

Thank you for being the first

reader, and for your

feedback.

To Jonathan

Thank you very much for

writing the foreword.

Contents

ACKNOWLEDGMENTS v

FOREWORD 13

PREFACE 17

INTRODUCTION 19

THE PURPOSE OF THIS BOOK 19

The Goal: Clarity and Empowerment in Your Career 20

A New Path Forward 21

Setting the Stage for Change 21

CHAPTER 1 24

THE PURPOSE OF RETHINKING 24

Why Re-evaluate Your Career? 24

Shifting Perspectives 24

The Power of Self-Redefinition 25

Exercise: Reflecting on Your Why 26

Exercise: Reflecting on What Matters 26

Looking Ahead 26

Setting the Stage for Rethinking 26

Building Clarity 27

Key Takeaways 28

CHAPTER 2 29

IDENTIFYING YOUR STRENGTHS 29

Understanding Your Unique Strengths 29

Natural Strengths vs. Learned Skills........ 29
Leveraging and Developing Your Strengths 30
Reflection Exercise................................ 30
Moving Forward with Confidence 31
Setting the Stage for Identification.......... 31
Reflections on Strength Discovery.......... 31
Key Takeaways: Identifying Your Strengths 32
CHAPTER 3.. 33
CAPTURING YOUR VALUES 33
The Role of Values in Career Satisfaction 33
Aligning Values with Career Goals 33
Emphasizing and Developing Your Core Values 34
Chapter Exercise.................................... 34
Building a Career That Honors Your Values 35
Setting the Stage for Your Values 35
Reflections on Values Exploration........... 36
Key Takeaways: Capturing Your Values . 37
CHAPTER 4.. 38
DEFINING WHAT YOU WANT TO WORK WITH 38
Imagining Your Ideal Skill Set................. 38
Balancing Current Skills with Areas for

Growth 38
Incorporating New Skills into Your Career Plan 39
Chapter Exercise 39
Bringing Your Skill Set to Life 40
Reflections on Future State 41
CHAPTER 5 43
NETWORKING AND RELATIONSHIP BUILDING 43
The Dual Role of Networking 44
Tailoring Networking to Your Style 44
Strategies for Introverts 45
Strategies for Extroverts 45
Why Tailoring Matters Now 45
Making Networking Sustainable 45
Chapter Exercises 46
Key Takeaways 47
• Networking is a natural part of refining your career vision - it strengthens your current foundation and expands opportunities for growth. 47
• Tailoring your networking style to your preferences ensures it feels authentic and sustainable. 47
CHAPTER 6 48
OVERCOMING OBSTACLES 48
Obstacles Within Your Control 48

Obstacles Outside Your Control 49

Chapter Exercises 52

Key Takeaways: Overcoming Obstacles. 53

CHAPTER 7 56

CLARIFYING WHAT YOU DON'T WANT TO WORK WITH 56

Defining Boundaries for a Healthier Career 56

Categorizing Activities, You'd Rather Avoid 56

Negotiable vs. Non-Negotiable Boundaries 57

Chapter Exercise 58

Moving Forward with Clarity 58

Reflections on Conscious Limitation........ 59

Key Takeaways: Clarifying What You Don't Want to Work With................................. 61

CHAPTER 8 62

ORGANIZING INTO THE THREE DIMENSIONS... 62

The Power of Defining Your Career Through Dimensions... 62

Creating Your Personal Career Map 63

Check the FAQ for how to download an A4 sized PDF of the Framework. 64

Chapter Exercise 65

Building a Career That Balances All Three

Dimensions 66

Reflections on Dimensional Insight 67

Key Takeaways from the Three Dimensions 68

CHAPTER 9 69

APPLYING THE MINDSET OF THE THREE DIMENSIONS 69

How to Put This Mindset into Action 71

Final Thoughts on Living the Framework. 73

CHAPTER 10 74

BUILDING YOUR CAREER BLUEPRINT 74

Turning Insights into Action 74

Balancing the Three Dimensions for Fulfillment 74

Setting Actionable Goals Based on Your Blueprint 75

Chapter Exercise 77

Living Your Blueprint 78

Reflections on Journey Quality 78

Key Takeaways: Your Career Blueprint... 80

CHAPTER 11 82

MANAGING TRANSITIONS 82

Transitions as Opportunities 82

Types of Transitions 83

Questions to Consider During a Transition 83

The Mindset of Adaptability 83
Adopting a Growth Mindset 84
CHAPTER 12 87
SUSTAINING GROWTH AND LEARNING 87
The Long-Term Benefits of the Framework 87
Key Benefits of Alignment 88
Revisiting and Realigning Goals 88
Strategies for Lifelong Growth 89
Chapter Exercises 90
Key Takeaways 91
CHAPTER 13 92
BUILDING YOUR CAREER PLAN 92
Turning Insight into Action 92
What to Include in Your Career Plan 92
CHAPTER 14 97
CONCLUSIONS 97
Your Career Plan: A Living Compass 97
The Value of Ongoing Self-Assessment 98
Moving Forward with Confidence and Purpose 98
APPENDIX A 100
FREQUENTLY ASKED QUESTIONS 100
My Career Plan 100
The Things Not Covered by the Book 102

APPENDIX B 103

EXAMPLES FOR SELECT CHAPTERS 103

Chapter 2: Your Strengths..................... 103

Chapter 3: Your Values 104

Chapter 4: What You Want to Work With 105

Chapter 8: The Three Dimensions......... 106

Chapter 10: Building Your Career Blueprint 107

Chapter 11: Managing Transitions......... 108

PROMO CODE 109

What's Next for You? 110

You Are the Key to Your Career's Next Chapter.. 110

Join The Movement.............................. 111

Copyrights and Used Resources 112

FOREWORD

First, I'm sorry for starting with a cheesy quote. But quotes don't become well-used and familiar without a grain of truth.

Socrates says, "The unexamined life is not worth living." This line appears in Plato's Apology, dramatizing Socrates' trial in 399 B.C.

If you use it well, this book will challenge you to examine your life and come back with something even more worthwhile.

I first met Henning Bech when he and I were matched as coach (me) and client (Henning) in a coaching demonstration for a private event connected to what was then called the World Business and Executive Coaches Summit (or WBECS, now called the coaching.com Summit).

WBECS gathers coaches from countries from all over the world, which explains how a coach from Cleveland, Ohio, ended up working with a client from Skåne County, Sweden. The WBECS organizers called with the invitation and said they would do all the organizing, and all I'd have to do is show up and coach. I quickly said, "Yes!"
This opportunity aligned beautifully with my mission. I believe in the power of coaching. Coaches adopt an attitude that challenges them to use their gifts, talents, experiences, training, background, and personality to improve their lives and the lives of the people around them. That's what coaches do when they work with clients.

So, Henning and I met and had a coaching conversation in front of a few dozen friends and colleagues. Afterward, the group processed what they observed, and I sat back and enjoyed the light bulbs turning on.

Henning told me later about his insights from the coaching. Over the next few months, he focused on coaching and challenged his colleagues to stretch themselves. I think (though I don't know for a fact) that our coaching conversation had something to do with Henning's decision to go out on his own and launch his full-time coaching practice.

That could have been the end of our connection, and one conversation would have been enough. But as the coaching world is small, Henning and I would occasionally cross paths. We'd see each other at online events, exchange pleasant hellos, and exchange emails.

Time passed. And what followed became a good example of what coaches call reflective practice.

First, one pauses regularly and reflects on what is happening in life, what you're learning, and what that learning means in the larger context.

Then, coaches who want to make the most of the opportunity find a conversation partner. (This person is called a "supervisor" in the coaching world.) The supervisor and coach discuss the key insights, realizations, and the application of those discoveries to coaching and life in general.

When Henning asked me to write a foreword to "The Pivotal Edge," my first response was to fire questions at him, as coaches do.

I started by asking, "What have you learned about yourself since our coaching session?" Henning then told me about the challenge of going out on his own, to which I responded, "How are you changing as a result of being on your own?"

A few minutes later, we discussed what Henning was hoping for from the next season of his coaching business. Maybe the most crucial question was, "How much of yourself have you captured in the pages of the book?"

Henning had thoughtful answers to all of these questions, and the book you hold (or see on your screen) results from Henning's application of his individual reflective practice. I know he's talked with others about his discoveries, and that process made what he offers to you better.

I'm excited by what he's accomplished; it will profoundly impact YOU if you let it. Building your career based on your giftedness, your sense of calling/mission, and the opportunities in front of you is a powerful opportunity for any of us.

He understands this and wants you to understand it as well. As he says in the first chapter, this book is built on the ©Dimensional Breakthrough Framework that Henning uses with his clients.

Here's my challenge: don't just read this book. Use the core ideas of reflective practice to bring it to life for yourself. After each chapter, take the coaching questions seriously.

Reflect on them privately and be as personal as you can in that reflection.

Work hard to put all those thoughts into your own words. Don't skimp on that.

Then, find someone you trust and talk about your discoveries. Work with that person in an ongoing partnership where you read the book together. As you read, reflect individually, and then discuss what you're discovering.

Or bring in a trusted someone to help you get beneath the surface of those individual reflections. Remember those questions that I put in front of Henning when he was thinking about writing this book:

- What are you learning about yourself?
- How are you changing as you reflect on your career?
- What do you want from the next season of your career?
- How much of yourself have you captured in the pages of the book?

Combining Henning's experienced insight with your individual or partnered reflective practice will take you to a place that becomes meaningful, powerful, and personal in unexpected ways.

That's my hope for you, and I suspect it's Henning's hope as well. Let the book affect you, but do the work as well. Don't just read it and put it on a shelf.

Read it, reflect on it, and then put it into action.

That aligns with who I know Henning to be and what I expect he's hoping you'll experience.

I hope you'll take his invitation seriously.

Jonathan Reitz
Cleveland, Ohio, USA
January 15, 2025

PREFACE

Every career journey is unique, yet the challenges we face often bind us in ways we don't expect.

Five years ago, I was coaching a colleague who felt stuck and overlooked in their career. Despite their brilliance and drive, they began to feel chained by self-doubt, unable to see a way forward.

That experience sparked a passion within me to help others avoid the same struggle - or find a way out of it. Over the years, I've worked with countless colleagues and clients, refining the framework that forms the backbone of this book. This isn't just a guide; it's a call to take charge of your career and align it with your values, aspirations, and purpose.

Taking the first step outside your comfort zone can feel daunting, but it's also the most rewarding. By working through the exercises in this book, you can gain the clarity, confidence, and tools to reshape your career into something deeply fulfilling.

For more than two decades as a leader, I've helped others succeed—professionally and personally. Working with clients across industries has shown me the transformative power of the model and its exercises. Each chapter will guide you with actionable exercises and real-world insights to help you unlock new perspectives and take the reins of your career.

This book is built on my ©Dimensional Breakthrough Framework that I use with clients. I have aimed at avoiding unnecessary detail while having a controlled level of repetition to mimic the coaching process in which I use the framework. All to ensure that you get as smooth an experience of the content as possible.

Redesigning your career requires effort, and with this book as your wingman you can stay on target and do it.

Your career transformation begins here. It's time to find your Pivotal Edge and step into a future of possibility and insight.

Enjoy!

Henning Bech

INTRODUCTION

THE PURPOSE OF THIS BOOK

In today's fast-paced globalized world, many find themselves swept along by the current of day-to-day demands, often losing sight of where their careers and lives are truly headed.

This book is an invitation to step back, take control, and purposefully chart a new path forward - one that resonates with who you are and what you want to accomplish. As we journey into the unknowns of career development, wisdom often begins from within.

"He who knows others is wise; he who knows himself is enlightened." – Lao Tzu

These words from Lao Tzu capture the essence of what we're here to do: to gain clarity deeper than just understanding the needs and expectations around you, by looking inward and connecting with what drives you at your core.

By understanding yourself, your strengths, values, and aspirations, you empower yourself to make meaningful choices, set boundaries, and pursue a path that aligns with your true purpose.

The Goal: Clarity and Empowerment in Your Career

This book provides a structured, reflective journey to help you see your career with fresh eyes. Whether you're feeling stuck, seeking new challenges, or aiming for a shift that feels more aligned with who you are, these chapters are here to guide you toward an empowered career perspective.

By turning your career upside down in reflection, we'll explore how to unlock a career path that is more successful and also deeply satisfying and meaningful.

Each chapter is designed to guide you through both learning and doing. You'll find exercises and reflections woven into the chapters that challenge your thinking, prompt honest assessment, and invite you to connect the concepts to your own career journey.

These moments of reflection are where real transformation begins - helping you clarify your strengths, values, aspirations, and boundaries.

Take your time with these exercises, as they're key to gaining clarity and taking charge of the direction, your career takes. This is your journey, and this book is here to empower you to write your own story.

A New Path Forward

It's easy to follow the paths of others or the expectations of the world around us. But true enlightenment, as Lao Tzu suggests, comes from knowing oneself.

Following the flow of the book will help you embrace that insight, gain clarity, and take deliberate action toward a more fulfilling career - one that you control, that aligns with who you truly are, and that brings the best of you to the world.

Setting the Stage for Change

To tune your mindset into embracing the process of this book I ask of you to start a journal, choose the format you find easiest to use, digital or pen and paper, and then write down or record your reflections to these questions and those of the following chapters.

All change requires you to step outside of your comfort zone, and it takes courage to begin.

You have this book in your hands and feel ready to dive right in - and it's fully understandable. But before you start, try these three reflections, and it's a promise that you will already be well on your way by doing just that!

- ? **What specific outcomes do I hope to achieve by rethinking my career?**

Even if no specific goals come to mind at first, reflect on small steps. It might be as simple as seeking more satisfaction in day-to-day work, reconnecting with a sense of purpose, or addressing frustrations. Starting there can help larger goals unfold naturally.

Once you have captured your goal(s) try to close your eyes

and imagine how your life will look once you have achieved your goal(s)!

Capture it in your journal and continue with the next reflection.

? **How ready am I to explore my career from new angles, and what fears or hesitations might hold me back?**

There are no good or bad answers to this question, and the key for you is to answer it as honestly as possible. This is your personal journey, and you'll want to make the most of it.

If you wonder how, you can quantify your readiness, you can always use a scale from 1 to 10, where 1 is "Not ready at all" and 10 is "I'm so ready, I'll explore from the top of a mountain if needed".

Exploring fears and hesitations is key to success, and the time spent will come in handy later when they show up on the journey as saboteurs trying to hold you back. You will be able to fence them off faster because you saw them coming.

? **What has kept me from examining my career more closely before, and how can a coach support me in addressing this?**

Understanding why that is, can help you reframe what you need for this journey to really take you where you want to be.

"I bought this book, and now you are telling me that I need a coach as well to make it happen!?"

This book is your guide, and you are fully capable of taking control by following it. But if you find yourself stuck or need a deeper dive, that's when a coach can help unlock what's beneath the surface.

Even without a coach you are not alone. Think of your journal as a companion on this journey. By reflecting regularly, you'll find clarity on the straightforward days and grounding on days that feel uncertain.

Remember, the reflections you begin with today may evolve over time. This is not a one-time exercise but rather a continuous practice of self-awareness that will serve you well throughout your career.

Trust yourself in this process - you have already taken the most important step simply by picking up this book and opening your mind to change.

CHAPTER 1

THE PURPOSE OF RETHINKING

Careers often take on lives of their own. We pursue promotions, chase milestones, and rarely pause to ask if the path aligns with who we are today.

Why Re-evaluate Your Career?

This chapter invites you to step off the well-worn road and view your career from a fresh perspective. By rethinking your career intentionally, you can uncover aspects of yourself and your work that may have been overlooked, which can then open doors to growth, higher satisfaction, and fulfillment.

Re-evaluation is a chance to explore available possibilities. Allow yourself to think big, dare to be bold, and refrain from dismissing ideas until you've thoroughly considered their potential. When reflecting, it's easy to say "no," especially when leaving your comfort zone. Challenge yourself to spend extra time evaluating options from the perspective of saying "yes," and you'll be surprised by the opportunities that will unfold.

Shifting Perspectives

Re-evaluating doesn't mean abandoning everything you've built. Instead, it's about giving yourself the freedom to look beyond titles and roles to view your career more holistically. This mindset shift allows new opportunities to emerge and encourages you to stay adaptable - not only to the demands of your field but to your personal and professional growth.

Careers used to be confined within a single profession. Today, they resemble a series of learning experiences, with growth often occurring across professions. Embracing these cross-disciplinary opportunities enriches your career and broadens your perspective.

The Power of Self-Redefinition

In rethinking your career, you redefine not only what you do but who you are and who you aim to become.

This process is empowering. You move from simply working to actively choosing a career path that highlights your strengths, aligns with your values, and brings the challenges you desire.

Taking ownership is liberating, and every achievement becomes more meaningful.

As Michelle Obama once said,

"Success is only meaningful and enjoyable if it feels like your own."

When you re-evaluate your career, you're taking charge and start to craft a work life that fits you, rather than squeezing yourself into a predefined context. This is about writing your own story.

Exercise: Reflecting on Your Why

Imagine this exercise as a conversation with yourself, free from judgment, pressure, or specific goals.

What do you hope to gain by examining your career with fresh eyes? What changes -big or small- could bring your career path closer to the one you envision for yourself?

Let your thoughts flow freely and record them in your journal. Highlight any ideas that stand out as potential actions.

Exercise: Reflecting on What Matters

Consider these questions: *What aspects of your work bring satisfaction? Where do you feel limited?*

Let these questions guide your reflections without pressure for definitive answers. This contemplation is a first step toward understanding what matters most to you.

Record your reflections in your journal and revisit them later to see how your perspectives may have evolved.

Looking Ahead

The journey of rethinking your career is about embracing possibility. You'll explore your strengths, values, and aspirations, aiming for a career that reflects both who you are today and who you strive to become.

Taking control of your career begins with seeing it as a journey you actively shape. Let this chapter's reflections lay the foundation for a future where you are the designer.

Setting the Stage for Rethinking

Embarking on change, expanding your comfort zone, or challenging the status quo can feel intimidating - or it can be an exciting expansion of your perspectives on topics like your capabilities, aspirations, and even your worries.

To avoid an overwhelming journey, it's helpful to start with a clear starting point, capturing honest and objective reflections in your journal. It's better to record "too much" than "too little." If you come across thoughts or details that don't quite fit into an exercise, note them down - they may connect later in the process.

Building Clarity

These clarity exercises are designed to help you understand what drives you towards change.

1. **What expectations or beliefs do I hold about my career that might benefit from a fresh perspective?**

This may connect to your comfort zone, past career choices that didn't serve you, or even internal "saboteurs" influencing your thinking.

2. **How would I describe my current career fulfillment, and where do I feel a sense of imbalance?**

This exercise encourages you to think about what prompted you to act. Not everything has to be negative; sometimes a generally positive outlook reveals imbalances that are worth addressing.

3. **What does a fulfilling career look like to me, and how can I clarify my vision?**

Here, establish your current view of what fulfillment means to you and explore areas where you need further clarity.

For now, don't focus on specific goals—this exercise is about understanding where you are today.

Key Takeaways

- **Career alignment begins with intentional reflection.** Stepping back allows you to evaluate whether your current path matches who you are today.
- **Possibilities arise when you challenge assumptions.** Allow yourself to think boldly and explore options without prematurely dismissing them.
- **Self-redefinition is empowering.** By actively shaping your career, you craft a work life that reflects your values and aspirations, rather than conforming to predefined expectations.

Coach's Corner

When coaching you within this chapter my focus is to stretch you and challenge your known perspectives. When you want something to change you need to do things in a new way, and it starts with getting new perspectives on what is.

An additional question to build on what you have already discovered could be:

"If you could completely start over in your career, with no fear of judgment or failure, what path would you choose, and why haven't you considered it until now?"

CHAPTER 2

IDENTIFYING YOUR STRENGTHS

Understanding Your Unique Strengths

In the daily rush of responsibilities, it's easy to lose sight of what truly makes us effective at work. Our strengths -those unique abilities that set us apart- are foundational to a fulfilling career. This chapter is about reconnecting with your core strengths and deciding how you want to use them moving forward.

Strengths often fall into two categories: those that feel natural, like second nature, and those we've honed over time through dedication and practice. Both types are invaluable, each serving us in different ways. By distinguishing between what comes naturally and what's been acquired, you gain a clearer understanding of how to use these strengths strategically as you shape your career.

Natural Strengths vs. Learned Skills

Some strengths seem to flow effortlessly and reflect who we are at a deeper level. These natural abilities often shine through, even when we take them for granted. Conversely, learned skills are those we've built through experience, training, and practice. These learned strengths demonstrate resilience and adaptability, adding depth and versatility to our professional lives.

Recognizing the difference between these types of strengths empowers you to make intentional decisions.

Perhaps a natural strength is something you want to lean into more, allowing it to guide your career choices. Alternatively, a learned skill may be valuable yet not as central to the direction you envision.

Leveraging and Developing Your Strengths

Identifying strengths is only the first step. It's equally important to determine which strengths you want to fully embrace and which you'd need to develop further.

Consider how each strength aligns with your career aspirations. Are there strengths that feel underutilized? Are there others that, while powerful, you'd like to place in the background? Embracing and refining these strengths can unlock new career paths and growth opportunities.

Reflection Exercise

Take a moment to list your strengths, both natural and learned. As you think about each one, consider how much you want it to shape your career moving forward. Rate each strength from 1 to 5, with 1 meaning you'd like to rely on it less and 5 meaning you want it to be a core part of your future.

This exercise is about alignment; there are no right or wrong answers, only an honest assessment of where you'd like your strengths to take you.

Through this process, you may discover strengths you've yet

to fully explore or skills that, while valuable, may no longer align with your vision.

Moving Forward with Confidence

By identifying, rating, and prioritizing your strengths, you're taking a powerful step toward a career that aligns with who you truly are. These strengths are the building blocks of your career journey, guiding you as you make choices that resonate with your values, goals, and aspirations.

Setting the Stage for Identification

Depending on how long you've been in your career, you likely have a broad set of strengths - some natural, some learned - that you need to evaluate. This process is best supported by detailed journaling, where you can capture both your strengths and your reflections on their significance.

Reflections on Strength Discovery

1. **What are my core strengths and are there any I may be underestimating or overlooking?**

This reflection helps you clarify your current view of your strengths, with a twist: try to identify those you might be underestimating or those that aren't on your radar yet.

2. **Which strengths do I wish to leverage more, and how do I integrate these into my future career?**

This exercise is about building an objective view of strengths you'd like more opportunities to use. Think about where you'd like to be challenged further and who can help you bring these strengths into play.

3. **How do my strengths align with my current role, and where could I use support in developing new skills?**

This foundational reflection explores how your current role allows you to exercise each strength. Consider what additional skills could broaden your versatility and align you with future goals.

Key Takeaways: Identifying Your Strengths

- **Recognizing strengths brings clarity.** Your unique abilities, both natural and learned, are the foundation for a fulfilling career.
- **Strengths guide intentional decisions.** Decide which strengths to emphasize or develop based on how they align with your future goals.
- **Growth happens when you leverage and refine.** Using your strengths strategically can unlock new directions and opportunities.

Coach's Corner

When coaching within this chapter my focus is to challenge you on conscious and unconscious decisions around what strengths you have and utilize.

An additional question to build on what you have already discovered could be:

"What is one strength you have been hesitant to embrace fully, and how might leaning into it change the trajectory of your career?"

CHAPTER 3

CAPTURING YOUR VALUES

The Role of Values in Career Satisfaction

Values are the compass that guide us, shaping our definitions of success, satisfaction, and purpose. While skills and strengths define what we *can* do, values determine *why* we do it. Knowing and honoring your values isn't just about feeling good at work; it's about creating alignment between what you do and what you believe in. When our values align with our work, they bring a deeper sense of fulfillment, purpose, and motivation that will allow you to perform at your best.

This chapter invites you to define your core values - the principles that are most meaningful to you and that you wish to bring into your career. By identifying and prioritizing these values, you lay the groundwork for decisions that truly resonate with who you are, building toward a more fulfilling journey.

Aligning Values with Career Goals

To achieve alignment, it's essential to consider which values you want to emphasize and how they connect with your future goals.

Just as we grow and evolve, so do our values. Some may feel timeless, while others might gain or lose significance as your career progresses. Take time to identify the values you wish to honor more fully and those you'd like to explore or refine as you move forward.

For example, integrity or creativity may have been constants throughout your career, while collaboration or innovation may be gaining importance as you explore new directions.

By naming and defining these values, you can approach your career from a place of authenticity, prioritizing what genuinely matters to you.

Emphasizing and Developing Your Core Values

Not all values apply equally in every role or at every stage of your career. Sometimes, certain values need to be at the forefront, guiding key decisions and helping you navigate challenges.

Other values may operate in the background, supporting rather than defining your actions. Knowing which values to emphasize and which to hold subtly can provide focus and clarity in your choices.

Chapter Exercise

List your core values, both personal and professional.

Reflect on each one and consider how it aligns with your career.

Which values do you want to prioritize or bring forward?

Are there any you'd like to explore more deeply or apply in new ways?

Use a scale from 1 to 5 to rate each value, with 1 indicating a desire to explore it further and 5 representing values that are already central to your career.

This exercise is about finding alignment and choosing values that will bring satisfaction and purpose to your path ahead.

Capture your reflections on this exercise in your journal.

Building a Career That Honors Your Values

By capturing and clarifying your values, you're laying the foundation for crossing "challenging waters" on your journey without being derailed to focus on things that will slow you down. The more aligned your work is with what you value, the more fulfilling and rewarding your career journey will be, and the easier it will be for you to make decisions.

In this way, you're not just building a career; you're shaping a path that reflects who you are and who you aim to become, and equally important, who you do not want to be.

Setting the Stage for Your Values

Values can make or break a career. Staying true to your values will influence how you plan your career and ultimately determine how successful you'll be in achieving your goals.

This might sound dramatic, but as you explore these exercises, aim to understand the depth of each value and its importance in your work life and why that is.

Reflections on Values Exploration

1. **What personal and professional values do I want my career to reflect?**

Begin by prioritizing which of your values are deeply rooted and integral to your entire journey, versus those you'd like to leverage or be challenged on in the coming phase.

2. **Where might I feel a conflict between my values and my current role or industry?**

Reflecting on this question can provide insight into areas where you may feel misalignment or friction, helping you understand why you may be seeking change. This clarity is key to taking control of your career.

3. **What will become possible for me when I align my values with my career?**

This reflection will help you visualize the potential benefits and the motivation that can drive your actions as you start tuning into your values and their role in shaping your career.

Capture your reflections on these exercises in your journal.

Key Takeaways: Capturing Your Values

- **Values are your career compass.** They guide your decisions and determine what brings meaning and fulfilment to your work.
- **Alignment with values boosts satisfaction.** Honouring what matters most to you leads to deeper purpose and motivation.
- **Defining your values is empowering.** Knowing and prioritizing your values sets the stage for authentic, intentional career choices.

Coach's Corner

When coaching within this chapter my focus is to help you understand when and how your Values are important or even existential to you.

An additional question to build on what you have already discovered could be:

"Which of your core values do you currently compromise the most in your career, and what would it take to stop doing so?"

CHAPTER 4

DEFINING WHAT YOU WANT TO WORK WITH

Imagining Your Ideal Skill Set

Your skills and experiences are the toolkit you bring to your career. They're not just a list of abilities; they shape what you can accomplish, how you're perceived, and where you can go. This chapter prompts you to take an honest look at your skills and talents, as well as the experiences you wish to gain, helping you create a career that's both dynamic and true to your goals.

As you think about what you want to work with in the future, balance the skills you have with those you'd like to acquire.

It's easy to overlook areas for growth, but investing in new skills can unlock pathways and bring fresh enthusiasm to your work. This process allows you to decide what to cultivate and what to introduce into your career plan, enabling you to build a future that reflects your aspirations.

Balancing Current Skills with Areas for Growth

Identifying the skills you want to use moving forward is about understanding both where you excel and where you wish to develop. Your current skills are strengths you can rely on, but they don't need to define your entire career. Look for opportunities to grow, to stretch yourself, and to add skills that align with your future vision. By combining these, you're creating a balanced skill set that is both stable and flexible.

Ask yourself: What skills and experiences would make your work more engaging? What would increase your effectiveness and allow you to bring greater value to your role? Understanding this balance between what you know and what you wish to learn helps you to map a career plan that encourages growth without losing sight of your strengths.

Incorporating New Skills into Your Career Plan

Once you know which skills you want to develop, it's time to think strategically about how to integrate them. New skills can come from various sources - courses, mentorship, hands-on experience, or new responsibilities. Set practical goals for skill-building and look for opportunities within your current role or network to gain the experience you need. Whether you're building expertise in a specific area or expanding your general skills, approaching your development with intention will set you up for sustainable, fulfilling growth.

Chapter Exercise

List your skills and experiences, both those you currently have and those you want to build.

For each skill, consider how it connects to your future career. What role do you see this skill playing?

Rate each skill on a scale of 1 to 5, with 1 being skills that are in early development and 5 being those that you have mastered and want to emphasize.

Think about how each skill supports your career goals and

where you may want to expand your capabilities.

Capture your reflections on this exercise in your journal.

A Note from Your Coach

When working with clients over time I have noticed that this is an area where your internal saboteurs will try to slow you down.

It's very easy to stall your decision making and slow your progress down; "I just need to get this certification before I can….", "I must build this skill before I'm ready…" and so on.

There will always be something that can prevent you from taking action and the best way forward with the clarity of your strengths, values and what you want to work with is to get perspective on what it would mean to you to achieve your goals and realize what you dream of.

And if you still feel stuck or just progressing in slow motion then a coach can help you.

Bringing Your Skill Set to Life

Your skill set isn't static - it's something you can shape, evolve, and grow with time. By clarifying the skills, you want to bring into your future, you're taking a thoughtful step toward creating a career that not only uses your strengths but also pushes you to expand.

With a well-rounded skill set, you're prepared to take on new challenges, adapt to change, and pursue a career that is both personally meaningful and professionally rewarding.

Reflections on Future State

1. **What skills or experiences am I passionate about bringing into my future career?**

Based on the chapter exercise make a prioritized list of the skills and experiences that you want to have a role in your future career.

2. **Are there any gaps between my current skill set and my aspirations that I might need support to fully ensure that I can close the gap?**

This exercise is about building knowledge on what you feel confident that you can identify and plan yourself, and what area(s) you might benefit from getting help on, for example from a coach.

Note: It doesn't mean that you can't progress without a coach. It means that you need to be objectively open to digging deeper into those areas.

3. **Which skills, even those I don't currently possess, feel essential to achieving my career goals?**

This exercise is about building perspective which can help you prioritize when you start building your career plan.

Capture your reflections on these exercises in your journal.

Coach's Corner

When coaching within this chapter my focus is to help you understand what fuels you, what makes you forget time and not least what you think is fun or believe would be fun if you tried it.

An additional question to build on what you have already learned about yourself could be:

"If you weren't limited by your current skills or experiences, what role or project would you pursue immediately?"

CHAPTER 5

NETWORKING AND RELATIONSHIP BUILDING

As your new career vision begins to take shape, networking naturally becomes a key part of the process.

Your professional relationships serve as bridges - both to reinforce the foundation of where you are now and to connect you to where you want to go. Strengthening existing relationships ensures you remain anchored in your current opportunities while maintaining trust and visibility with those who know you well.

At the same time, building new connections is essential to aligning with your evolving goals. As your perspective broadens and your vision crystallizes, reaching out to those who can support, mentor, or inspire you will open doors to opportunities you may not have considered yet.

This chapter provides actionable strategies for maintaining your current network and expanding it in ways that align with your future state.

Whether you thrive in smaller, intentional interactions or are energized by social dynamics, this chapter offers insights and ways to help you navigate networking effectively.

The Dual Role of Networking

Networking isn't an isolated task - it's a natural extension of your evolving career vision. As you begin to define what matters most in your next steps, your network plays a dual role:

1. **Strengthening Current Connections**
Your existing professional relationships serve as a stable foundation. These are the people who know your strengths and can advocate for you as you grow. Maintaining these connections is about nurturing trust and visibility - critical factors when transitioning or pursuing new opportunities.

2. **Building New Connections**
As your vision solidifies, expanding your network is essential. New relationships can expose you to fresh perspectives, industries, or opportunities that align with your aspirations.

By intentionally connecting with those who can support your future state, you set the stage for growth. Support can have many shapes, sometimes you just want to Follow them on LinkedIn to learn from their posts, sometimes you want to talk, or maybe you are looking for a mentor etc.

Tailoring Networking to Your Style

Networking at this stage is about aligning your efforts with your evolving goals, but regardless of why you connect with someone, be your authentic self and honest on why you want to connect and get to know each other before you present eventual big asks.

Whether you're strengthening existing relationships or forging new ones, your personality and preferences will shape how you engage.

Strategies for Introverts

- Focus on quality over quantity: Engage deeply with a few key individuals who align with your vision.
- Use digital tools: Platforms like LinkedIn or email provide low-pressure ways to connect meaningfully.
- Prepare with purpose: Knowing your goals for an event or conversation can help ease the experience.

Strategies for Extroverts

- Leverage social energy: Use events, conferences, or group settings to connect widely and identify mutual interests.
- Share your vision with those you want to support you: Clearly communicate your evolving career goals to spark meaningful conversations.
- Follow through: Extroverts excel at initial connections but should focus on maintaining relationships long-term.

Why Tailoring Matters Now

As your vision takes shape, the way you network will help you test and refine it. Conversations with trusted connections or new contacts can validate ideas, reveal hidden opportunities, or highlight gaps in your thinking.

Making Networking Sustainable

Networking is not just a box to check - it's an ongoing process. At this stage, it's about balancing your current connections with the new relationships that will help your career forward.

Consistent, intentional actions are the key to keeping your network vibrant and aligned with your evolving goals.

Chapter Exercises

1. **Map Your Current Network**

Create a list of key professional relationships. Note how these connections currently support your career and identify 2-3 people you'd like to reconnect with to maintain trust and visibility.

2. **Plan Two New Connections**

Reflect on your career vision and consider which areas require new relationships. Identify specific people or roles to target and outline how you will reach out, through events, LinkedIn, or introductions from mutual contacts.

Key Takeaways

- Networking is a natural part of refining your career vision - it strengthens your current foundation and expands opportunities for growth.
- Tailoring your networking style to your preferences ensures it feels authentic and sustainable.
- Maintaining consistency in your networking efforts will keep you aligned with your evolving goals.

A Note from Your Coach

When working with clients I have noticed that Networking is an area where it's easy to avoid taking action because of what you think you can or can't do. "Can I ask for help even that I can't see how I can help them back?"

An important lesson I've learned over the years is that often when you receive help you see it as a big thing because you need the help, and the giver often see it as a small thing when it's trivial to them, and most people will help you if they can see that you help others, "pay it forward" is a well used concept that will help you.

If you want to start take action on Networking then ask yourself a question like: "If your career depended on a single conversation, who would you reach out to, and why haven't you made that connection yet?" can be helpful to see perspective.

CHAPTER 6

OVERCOMING OBSTACLES

As you work toward your career goals, obstacles are inevitable. Some will be internal, like fear of failure or self-doubt. Others will be external, such as organizational barriers or economic shifts. This chapter equips you to face both kinds of challenges with clarity, confidence, and resilience.

At this stage, the work you've done in the previous chapters -defining your values, strengths, and career vision- becomes a powerful resource. By leveraging the process in this book, you'll be better prepared to navigate obstacles, including those outside your control.

Obstacles Within Your Control

Internal obstacles often stem from mindset challenges, like fear of failure or imposter syndrome. While these barriers can feel overwhelming, they're within your control to address.

Common Internal Obstacles:

- **Fear of Failure:** A fear of making mistakes can paralyze progress. Sometimes this is triggered by the work environment, but taking action is still within your control.

- **Imposter Syndrome:** Feeling undeserving of success can hold you back from seizing opportunities.
- **Overthinking:** Getting stuck in analysis paralysis prevents action.

Strategies to Overcome Internal Obstacles:

- Reframe failure as a learning opportunity. Instead of asking, "What if I fail?" ask, "What can I learn if this doesn't go as planned?"
- When you feel undeserving. Instead of asking "What have I done to deserve this?" ask, "What is the worst thing that can happen if I just say 'thank you' and embrace the opportunity/the praise/the raise/etc?"
- When you experience analysis paralysis. Instead of asking, "What if something I didn't plan for happen?" ask, "What opportunities or positive outcomes would be possible if I take action right now!?"
- Practice self-compassion by acknowledging that growth comes with discomfort, and that embracing discomfort will help not only your growth but also your ability to make decisions simply because you can focus on what's doable instead of what obstacles you face.
- Set realistic and meaningful milestones to create momentum and build confidence and motivation to achieve them.

Obstacles Outside Your Control

External obstacles often arise from circumstances beyond your influence, such as changes in industry trends, workplace culture, or organizational policies. While you can't always control these factors, you can control how you respond to them.

Examples of External Obstacles:

- **Industry Shifts:** Economic changes or evolving technologies can disrupt career plans.
- **Workplace Culture:** Misalignment with company values or leadership can create frustration.
- **Lack of Opportunities:** Limited growth paths in your current role or organization.

Strategies for Managing External Obstacles:

- Stay proactive by keeping your skills and network up to date. Spend 25% of your educational efforts on a mix of something for the future and something that you are passionate about. This positions you to pivot quickly if needed.
- Focus on what you can influence, such as improving your visibility or building connections in new industries. With the effort you are putting into building insights on yourself using this book you will also know what to influence to serve your career perspective.
- Use setbacks as opportunities to revisit and refine your career vision. Identify what caused the setback and check if you need to revise actions around education or training.

Turning Obstacles into Opportunities

Obstacles, whether internal or external, often contain hidden opportunities. A challenge can force you to explore new directions, build resilience, or discover strengths you didn't know you had. Anything that takes you outside your comfort zone has potential to reveal something positive that you didn't think of yourself or areas you will benefit from strengthening.

Reframing Challenges – The Power of Your Internal Language

The way we speak to ourselves has a significant impact on how we perceive and tackle obstacles. Internal language - the silent dialogue that shapes our thoughts - can either empower us to move forward or hold us back in fear and doubt.

When we encounter challenges, our internal language often defaults to questions like:

- "Why is this happening to me?"
- "What if I fail?"
- "I can't handle this."

This kind of language feeds into a mindset of limitation and discouragement, making obstacles seem bigger than they are.

But what happens when we shift the narrative? Consider reframing using these questions:

- "What can I learn from this?"

- "What steps can I take to navigate this?"
- "Who or what can support me in overcoming this?"

This shift in language turns obstacles into opportunities for growth and problem-solving. Instead of focusing on the obstacle itself, you start focusing on solutions, possibilities, and resilience.

- Instead of seeing obstacles as roadblocks, view them as steps in your journey.
- Reflect on how past challenges have shaped your growth and what they taught you about yourself.

Example on reframing:

Original thought: "This is too hard; I'll never figure it out."

Reframed thought: "This is a chance to develop a new skill, when take it one step at a time."

Building Your "Obstacle Toolkit"

- Create a plan for handling setbacks, such as who you'll lean on for support and what steps you'll take to regroup.
- Document lessons learned from each challenge to apply them to future situations.

Chapter Exercises

1. Obstacle Reframing

Reflect on a current or past challenge. Reframe it by asking yourself:

"What opportunity did this obstacle create for growth or alignment with my values?"

2. **Your Obstacle Toolkit**

Prepare for future challenges by identifying:

- Three internal obstacles (e.g., fear, self-doubt) and three external obstacles (e.g., organizational issues, market changes).
- For each obstacle, list one actionable strategy or resource to help you navigate it effectively.

3. **Reframing Your Internal Dialogue**

Practice shifting your mindset with this step-by-step exercise:

1. Recall a recent obstacle or challenge.
2. Write down the first thoughts that came to mind when you faced it.
3. Rewrite those thoughts using empowering language, focusing on:
    - What you can do.
    - What you can learn.
    - How you can grow.

Key Takeaways: Overcoming Obstacles

1. **Obstacles Are Inevitable**

Challenges, both internal and external, are a natural part of your career journey. Recognizing them as opportunities rather than threats is the first step to overcoming them.

2. **Leverage Your Resources**

The values, strengths, and career vision you've defined in earlier chapters provide a solid foundation for navigating obstacles with clarity and confidence.

3. **Internal Obstacles Are Within Your Control**

Mindset challenges like fear of failure, imposter syndrome, and overthinking can be addressed by:

- Reframing failure as a learning opportunity.
- Practicing self-compassion and patience.
- Setting realistic milestones to build confidence and momentum.

4. **External Obstacles Require Strategic Responses**

Challenges beyond your control, such as industry shifts or workplace misalignment, can be managed by:

- Staying proactive with skill development and networking.
- Focusing on what you can influence.
- Viewing setbacks as opportunities to refine your career vision.

5. **Your Internal Language Shapes Your Approach**

- The way you speak to yourself during challenges determines whether obstacles feel insurmountable or manageable.
- Reframing negative self-talk into empowering questions helps shift focus from limitations to solutions and

possibilities.

6. **Obstacles Often Contain Hidden Opportunities**

Each challenge offers a chance to grow, discover new strengths, and build resilience. Reflect on how past obstacles have shaped your growth to fuel confidence in the future.

Coach's Corner

When coaching within this chapter my focus is to help you adapt to a Growth Mindset even when things do not go as you planned.

An additional question to build on what you have already discovered could be:

"What is the biggest fear you have about failing in your career, and how might facing it directly unlock new opportunities for growth?"

CHAPTER 7

CLARIFYING WHAT YOU DON'T WANT TO WORK WITH

Defining Boundaries for a Healthier Career

In the pursuit of career growth, it's easy to focus solely on what you want to achieve and the skills you aim to develop. Yet, knowing what you want to avoid is just as critical.

By defining what you don't want to work with - the tasks, roles, or skills that drain you - you establish clear boundaries. These boundaries allow you to steer your career in a direction that not only aligns with your strengths but also respects your personal well-being and preferences.

This chapter encourages you to be honest about what doesn't serve you, guiding you through a process to evaluate which tasks and roles to minimize or avoid entirely. When you clarify these areas, you give yourself the freedom to build a career that elevates you, rather than one that depletes your energy or limits your potential.

Categorizing Activities, You'd Rather Avoid

There are probably tasks you're good at but would prefer not to do. These may be skills you've picked up along the way -

tasks you can complete effectively but they drain your energy or distract you from more fulfilling aspects of your work.

Identifying these activities helps you to create a more intentional career path. You will still experience situations where you have to “take one for the team” because you have the needed skill but being aware of what you’d rather avoid makes it easier to decide on future roles.

You’re not just focusing on what you do well; you’re choosing where to apply your strengths with purpose.

Consider which activities you’d rather avoid and categorize them by importance. This isn’t about rejecting tasks outright; it’s about understanding your preferences and being mindful of how you allocate your time and energy.

Negotiable vs. Non-Negotiable Boundaries

Not every task is avoidable but distinguishing between negotiable and non-negotiable aspects of your work can empower you to make better choices when evaluating an opportunity.

Perhaps there are tasks that, while not ideal, you’re open to perform under certain conditions. Others may be clear “no-go’s” for your future career.

By defining which elements are negotiable and which are absolute, you set yourself up for more being able to have more satisfying roles, knowing where you’re willing to compromise and where you’re not. Sometimes it will also make it clear why you can’t continue in a role when the personal “cost” outweighs the benefit of staying.

Chapter Exercise

List the tasks, skills, or roles you'd like to avoid, and categorize each into one of three groups:

1. **Don't want to and will not do**: These are non-negotiable boundaries—activities you're unwilling to engage in going forward.
2. **Good at but don't want to**: Tasks that you can handle really well but prefer to avoid, as they don't contribute to your desired career path or satisfaction.
3. **Negotiable**: These are activities you may not prefer but are willing to do under certain conditions.

This exercise helps you set clear, practical boundaries, making it easier to identify roles and opportunities that align with what you truly want.

Capture your reflections on this exercise in your journal.

Moving Forward with Clarity

By clarifying what you don't want to work with, you're empowering yourself to pursue roles that energize and inspire you. These boundaries aren't limitations - they're tools to help you create a career that respects both your strengths and your well-being.

Putting in the effort now will make it easier to evaluate even small opportunities in your daily work. This is not to advocate that you make a hard stop on executing things you don't want to do – we all have commitments that we can't just drop, but when you're prepared to have a dialogue about it, you'll be surprised how often there are possibility for making changes.

What you don't want to do might be on top of other people's

want to do list, and silently accepting a task you don't like will just lead to dissatisfaction.

When preparing yourself for dialogue and for making choices, you pave the way for a career that feels both fulfilling and sustainable, setting yourself up for long-term satisfaction and success that is sustainable. It requires the insights you are building and taking action on them.

Reflections on Conscious Limitation

Based on the chapter exercise

1. **What made a task, role or activity classify as a non-negotiable boundary?**

This exercise is about understanding what impact it has on you when you must do something you for example find draining or demotivating. Once you understand that, it becomes clear what the benefits are when you eradicate or minimize them in your career going forward!?

2. **How do I know if my negotiable boundaries are valuable to the person or company I'm negotiating with? And what conditions need to be met for me to bring them into a negotiation?**

Preparation is key, and this exercise should be repeated every time you face a new type of negotiation. This is about knowing your value - else it becomes a bargaining chip which will just increase your scope without you getting something in return.

3. **How will I communicate my boundaries effectively in a professional setting?**

This exercise will help you when you are faced with someone who knows that you are good at something specific, but you don't want to do it, and it might even be one of your non-negotiables. Preparation on how to respond without placing yourself in a corner or giving up easily on a boundary.

Capture your reflections on these exercises in your journal.

Coach's Corner

When coaching on what you don't want my focus is to help you identify what is within your control to define, and what opportunities you have to exercise that control, and what it would give you or cost you.

An additional question to build on what you have already discovered could be:

"If you could completely remove one aspect of your current role or career, what would it be, and what's stopping you from doing so?"

Key Takeaways: Clarifying What You Don't Want to Work With

- **Boundaries create clarity.** Understanding what you don't want allows you to focus on roles and tasks that energize and inspire you.
- **Negotiate with purpose.** Identifying negotiable and non-negotiable boundaries empowers you to make intentional choices.
- **Saying "no" is part of growth.** Setting limits helps you build a career that respects your well-being and aligns with your values.

CHAPTER 8

ORGANIZING INTO THE THREE DIMENSIONS

The Power of Defining Your Career Through Dimensions

By now, you've examined your strengths, values, aspirations, and boundaries. The next step is to bring these insights together into a unified vision for your career.

This chapter introduces the powerful Dimensional Breakthrough Framework for organizing your career goals into three essential dimensions: the **Core of You**, the **Core of Challenge**, and the **Core of Purpose**. Each dimension represents a unique aspect of your professional life, helping you create a holistic career map that honors your personal identity, growth ambitions, and overarching purpose.

Defining Each Dimension

1. **Core of You**: This dimension is about alignment with your core values and the personal qualities that define you. It includes the strengths and values that are integral to who you are. Think of this as the foundation of your career—what makes you feel true to yourself, grounded, and motivated.
2. **Core of Challenge**: Here, we explore the areas where you seek growth, development, and challenge. This dimension isn't about comfort; it's about pushing your

boundaries and building new skills. Whether it's taking on a complex project or stepping into a new role, the Core of Challenge represents the aspects of your career that stretch you.

3. **Core of Purpose**: This dimension reflects your desire to create meaning, contribute, and make an impact. It includes the goals and activities that align with your vision of purpose, guiding you toward a career that not only fulfills but also inspires you. The Core of Purpose is about finding work that resonates with your deeper "why."

Creating Your Personal Career Map

With these three dimensions in mind, you can begin to organize your career around the principles of personal alignment, growth, and purpose.

By mapping your strengths, values, and preferences into these dimensions, you'll create a visual representation of your ideal career path. This map helps you balance stability, challenge, and meaning, allowing each dimension to support the others for a fulfilling, sustainable career.

How the Dimensional Breakthrough Framework differs from most other career frameworks is that it is not aimed at just getting you ready for a specific job or role. What I intend to help you build is a new mindset, a new pair of looking glasses to alter how your think about and plan your career vision.

It's aimed at building so strong insight on yourself that you will know what you can do besides an individual job or role and make it easier to differentiate yourself when applying for a job or a role, and at the same time have a clear perspective on how it can contribute to your overall career progress.

Check the FAQ for how to download an A4 sized PDF of the Framework.

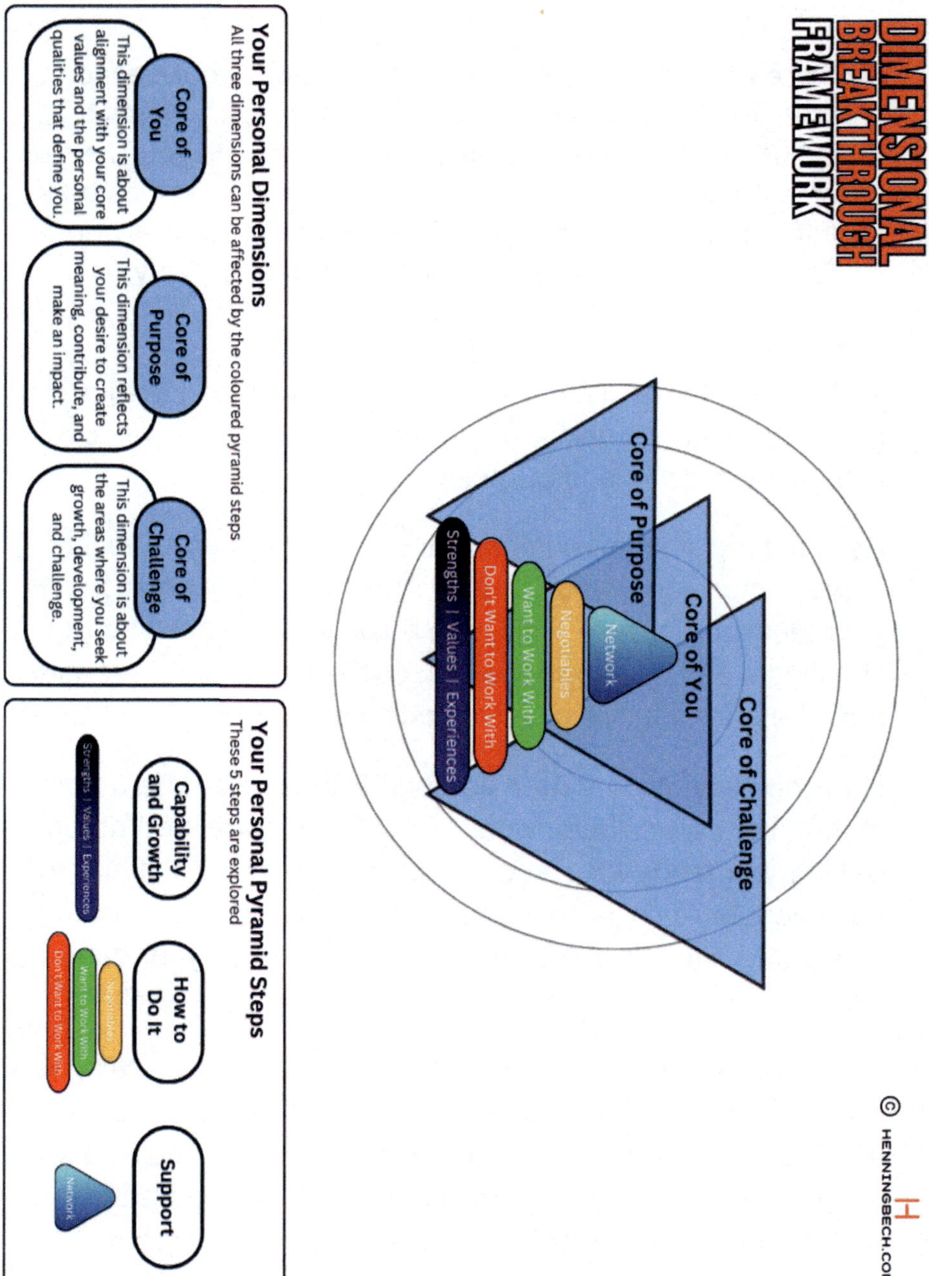

Chapter Exercise

The visual representation of this different mindset is an upside down pyramid shape for each of the Dimensions.

As you work through this exercise, draw 3 upside-down pyramids on some pieces of paper or in your preferred digital tool. One for each Dimension.

Take each of the insights you've gathered—strengths, values, skills, and preferences—and map them into one or more of the dimensions:

1. **Core of You**: Which strengths, values, or activities are essential to your personal alignment?
2. **Core of Challenge**: What skills or areas of growth do you want to pursue to stretch and develop yourself?
3. **Core of Purpose**: What goals or activities resonate with your sense of purpose and vision?

Some elements may fit neatly into one dimension, while others might overlap. This exercise is about finding the right balance for you, so feel free to experiment with where each piece belongs.

As you map to the Dimensions, have all the most important elements closer to the pointy part of the pyramids and the less important elements and the negotiables at the broader part at the top.

This is an important part of the mindset building so take your time to evaluate the importance each element has in each Dimension you represent it in. In the next chapter I will describe how you apply the mindset.

Building a Career That Balances All Three Dimensions

By organizing your career into these three dimensions, you create a balanced framework that reflects who you are, where you want to grow, and what you aspire to achieve.

This holistic approach not only supports your immediate goals but also sets you up for long-term satisfaction and success.

As you move forward, this map can serve as a guide, reminding you of your personal alignment, areas for growth, and the purpose which drives your journey.

Having a balanced framework will make it easier for you to build your career plan.

A Note from Your Coach

It's very easy to be pulled into an internal blame-game on things you realize could have been different, but I recommend that you park it – if you need, make a note of it for eventual later re-visit – and keep your focus and attention on the Dimensions.

Primarily, because you can't change what has already been done, and you are following this book to change your approach.

Reflections on Dimensional Insight

Based on the chapter exercise

1. **What elements of my career most align with who I am, and how can I strengthen these to become who I want to be?**

This exercise can be a little different depending on whether you want to grow your current career perspective or if you are looking to completely reinvent yourself professionally. Complete reinvention tends to have more focus on what you need to build than how to strengthen something you already possess.

2. **What growth challenges am I ready to take on, and where might I feel resistance?**

This is a key exercise, as you reflect on this question you will encounter some of your internal "saboteurs" that will try to persuade you to maintain status quo.

This is perfectly normal when you have to go outside your comfort zone, or just consider making changes. Here you will have the benefit of the initial work you did in the Introduction exercises so consult your journal and see what reflections you had on "saboteurs".

3. **How might a coach help me find purpose-driven opportunities that fit my values and strengths?**

This book can absolutely get you to where you need to be without a coach, but where a coach can come in handy is challenging your thinking with added depth and fast-tracking your process. This is what I do when I help clients with their careers using the method from this book.

Key Takeaways from the Three Dimensions

- **The Three Dimensions create balance.** Align the Core of You, Core of Challenge, and Core of Purpose to design a career that feels complete.
- **Each dimension has a role.** Your core values ground you, challenges drive growth, and purpose brings meaning to your work.
- **Mapping dimensions unlocks clarity.** Organizing your strengths, aspirations, and goals within these dimensions supports intentional career decisions.

Coach's Corner

When coaching within this chapter my focus is to help you identify what potential you haven't realized, what might be holding you back, and build perspective on what is key for you to address.

An additional question to build on what you have already discovered could be:

"Which of the three dimensions: Core of You, Core of Challenge, or Core of Purpose do you currently feel least aligned with, and how is that affecting your overall fulfillment?"

CHAPTER 9

APPLYING THE MINDSET OF THE THREE DIMENSIONS

The upside-down pyramids you created in Chapter 8 are more than a framework - they represent a shift in how you view your career. Instead of just asking, "Do I meet the requirements?" your new perspective should make you ask, "How does this role align with who I am, what I want to grow into, and the impact I aim to create?"

This approach widens your field of vision. It allows you to evaluate jobs, roles, and opportunities based on facts about your strengths, values, and negotiables. Here's an adaptable guide on how you can apply this mindset in practical ways.

1. See Beyond Job Descriptions

With the upside-down pyramids, you're no longer constrained by a narrow, requirement-based view of opportunities. Instead:

- Core of You gives you clarity about what you naturally bring to the table—your strengths, values, and unique skills.
- Core of Challenge highlights areas where you're ready to grow, showing opportunities to stretch your

abilities rather than just maintain the status quo.
- Core of Purpose ensures you're thinking beyond the job itself to how it contributes to your long-term vision.

Mental Shift: Stop focusing solely on "checking all the boxes" in a job description. Instead, consider how the role can align with your dimensions and where you can bring something unique that the role may not explicitly require.

2. Approach Opportunities as a Two-Way Street

The framework empowers you to see opportunities not just as something to apply for, but as something to negotiate with:

- **What You Bring**: Use your dimensions to articulate what you can offer that goes beyond the job description. For example, a strength from the Core of You or an area of expertise that aligns with the Core of Challenge can make you stand out.

- **What You Need**: Know your negotiables. Use your pyramids to identify areas where the opportunity must align with your values (e.g., work-life balance, leadership style, or growth potential).

Mental Shift: Start viewing roles as mutual value exchanges. Instead of trying to fit into a role, evaluate how well the role fits you and how you can shape it to align with your dimensions.

3. Broaden Your Vision of Career Paths

When you use the upside-down pyramids, new possibilities emerge:

- Roles or industries you hadn't considered may now

seem viable because they align with your Core of You and provide meaningful growth in your Core of Challenge.

- Non-traditional opportunities like project-based work, consulting, or leadership in unfamiliar fields may align with your Core of Purpose in unexpected ways.

Mental Shift: Expand your horizons by asking, "What can this opportunity become when seen through the lens of my three dimensions?"

4. Make Clearer Decisions Faster

The pyramids act as a decision-making compass:

- Evaluate how each dimension is supported or stretched by the opportunity.
- Ask, "Does this role respect my values, offer meaningful growth, and contribute to my purpose?"
- Use these insights to weigh your options more confidently and avoid analysis paralysis.

Mental Shift: Instead of agonizing over whether an opportunity is "right," use your pyramids to determine how well it fits into your broader career goals.

How to Put This Mindset into Action

Here are some practical ways to start applying the upside-down pyramids in your career:

1. Prepare for Conversations and Negotiations

Whether you're discussing a new role or a career change, bring your dimensions into the conversation:

- Highlight strengths from your **Core of You** that

uniquely position you for the role.

- Emphasize areas in your **Core of Challenge** where you're eager to grow, showing a proactive mindset.
- Advocate for elements that align with your **Core of Purpose** (e.g., flexible working arrangements, alignment with long-term goals).

2. Broaden Your Research

When evaluating opportunities, go beyond the surface:

- Research companies and roles with your pyramids in mind. Does their culture align with your **Core of You**?
- Look for roles that offer growth challenges in areas you've identified in your **Core of Challenge**.
- Explore how each opportunity supports your **Core of Purpose**—does it contribute to your vision, or is it just a steppingstone?

3. Rethink "Traditional" Career Metrics

The mindset helps you move beyond traditional success metrics (e.g., title, salary, location) to more meaningful measures of alignment:

- Does this opportunity make you feel energized and aligned with your **Core of You**?
- Will it stretch your skills without overwhelming you, aligning with your **Core of Challenge**?
- Does it offer purpose and meaning that fits into your bigger picture of **Core of Purpose**?

Exercises for Building This Mental Shift

1. **Opportunity Mapping**:
   - For any new role or project, create a mini pyramid and map how it fits into each dimension. What does it offer, and what might you need to negotiate?
2. **Strength-Based Reflection**:
   - List 2-3 strengths from your **Core of You** and practice framing them as unique contributions during interviews or networking.
3. **Purpose Alignment Check**:
   - Before saying "yes" to an opportunity, ask: "Does this bring me closer to the career I envision, or is it a detour?"

Final Thoughts on Living the Framework

The mental shift of the upside-down pyramids helps you see your career from a new perspective. It broadens your options, empowers you to negotiate based on what matters to you, and ensures you're making intentional, aligned decisions and not just trying to match a list of requirements.

By applying this mindset, you'll approach your career with clarity, confidence, and control, with potential to turn every opportunity into a step forward. I'm confident that when you start living this mindset you will never want to go back to "the old way".

CHAPTER 10

BUILDING YOUR CAREER BLUEPRINT

Turning Insights into Action

With a clear understanding of your strengths, values, preferences, and purpose, you're ready to take the next step: building a career blueprint that aligns with who you are and where you want to go. This chapter guides you in transforming your insights into a strategic, actionable plan.

By blending the three dimensions, Core of You, Core of Challenge, and Core of Purpose - you'll create a roadmap that is not only practical but also deeply meaningful.

This blueprint is more than just a career plan; it's a dynamic guide designed to evolve with you.

It's about making intentional choices that align with your vision of fulfillment, growth, and impact. By setting actionable goals, you bring each dimension into harmony, creating a balanced path that supports both your personal satisfaction and professional development.

Balancing the Three Dimensions for Fulfillment

Each dimension of your career, Core of You, Core of Challenge, and Core of Purpose contributes to a different facet of fulfillment. When balanced, these dimensions work together to create a career that feels complete and rewarding. For example:

- **Core of You** ensures you stay connected to what makes you feel authentic and grounded.
- **Core of Challenge** encourages continuous learning and pushes you to achieve new heights.
- **Core of Purpose** keeps you focused on making a meaningful impact.

Note! Balancing these dimensions doesn't mean giving each equal weight at all times.

Instead, it's about understanding when and where to focus your energy. For instance, you might prioritize growth (Core of Challenge) when taking on a new role, while emphasizing purpose (Core of Purpose) when leading a team or contributing to a project that aligns with your vision. A balanced career is flexible and adaptive, reflecting your needs at different stages.

Setting Actionable Goals Based on Your Blueprint

With a balanced vision in mind, it's time to set clear, actionable goals for each dimension. Goals bring your blueprint to life, turning abstract values and strengths into tangible steps. Consider each dimension and set specific objectives that are realistic yet challenging and motivating.

These goals should challenge you while remaining achievable within the framework of a 1–3-year career plan.

When setting goals:

- **For the Core of You**, focus on objectives that reinforce alignment with your values and core strengths, like finding roles that honor your principles or prioritizing tasks that align with your natural talents.
- **For the Core of Challenge**, identify growth opportunities that stretch your abilities, such as skill development, new responsibilities, or professional certifications.
- **For the Core of Purpose**, set goals that connect your work to a larger vision, like leading initiatives that create positive change, mentoring others, or taking on roles with meaningful impact.

A Note from Your Coach

Make sure that you do not define actions so complex that they are close to impossible to complete.

One of the things I see new clients struggle with is actually completing the actions they have defined.

This mostly has to do with one of these two reasons:

1. There are several things to complete in each action and this often prevents transparency of progress which is damaging to both your motivation and your execution.
2. The other, and very common, reason is that the actions are not the ones you need. Only spend time on actions that will make a difference to you.

If you struggle with progress, challenge your thinking and if still stuck, contract a coach to help you uncover what is holding you back from progressing.

Chapter Exercise

Based on the insights you've gathered, draft a 1-3 year plan that aligns with your newly defined career objectives. For each dimension, set at least one goal that connects with your blueprint:

1. **Core of You**: What specific roles or actions will help you stay grounded in your values and strengths?
2. **Core of Challenge**: What skill development or growth opportunities will drive your progress and keep you engaged?
3. **Core of Purpose**: What goals or projects will bring you closer to your long-term vision?

Think of this as a flexible plan, with room to adapt as you gain new insights and encounter new opportunities.

Writing down your goals not only clarifies your direction but also provides a roadmap for moving forward with confidence and purpose.

As you write down your goals it's important to define the time perspective of your goals as well as capture eventual known dependencies.

Getting clarity on the time perspective will be helpful when you start to define the actions needed to achieve each goal, and later on, understanding the time perspective and eventual constraints is a pre-requisite for a successful completion of an action.

Living Your Blueprint

As you bring this blueprint to life, remember that it's a tool for reflection and guidance. Your career journey may take unexpected turns, but by staying true to the dimensions you've defined, you can adapt and grow while staying connected to your values and purpose.

Your blueprint will serve as a reminder of what matters most, helping you navigate changes, seize opportunities, and build a career that genuinely reflects who you are.

Unexpected turns in your career frequently show up as opportunities you could not plan for. When they do, evaluate if taking an opportunity will support your goals or even fast-track them without negative impact on your Core.

Do not write off opportunities without reflection, utilize all the knowledge about yourself you have gathered in your journal to make informed decisions, adapt and grow and then update your plan where needed.

Reflections on Journey Quality

1. **What are my top priorities over the next 2-3 years, and how do they align with each dimension?**

Chances are that you will have a longer list of goals and activities you want to prioritize, which is great if you can stay focused on those most important to you for the next 2-3 years!

This exercise is about sorting the list to make sure that you do not put too much on your plate at the same time. Think of the list as a buffet you pick from, if you put too much on your plate then some of it will be left cold.

You can always "go for seconds" so start with a list of priorities that are balancing the edge between a good challenge, a stretch and too much. If it's not ambitious you will not give it your best, or you might not have uncovered your true top priorities!?

Reflecting on how they align with your dimensions will support you in following your blueprint and adjust where needed.

2. **How comfortable am I setting actionable goals, and where might I benefit from coaching support?**

Any dream and any goal will stay as just that if you do not put action behind them. A good actionable goal is an outcome that you can specifically define the key components of and put a time perspective on.

Be as specific as needed to know what to achieve, but not so detailed that you have no flexibility to adapt to opportunities without having to revisit your plan all the time.

As you work on defining your actionable goals you might experience that your inner saboteurs try to "help" you play it safe. Consult your journal and what you wrote on saboteurs that you anticipated to see if you already know how to fence them off.

If that doesn't help you forward, then you might benefit from coaching support to reinforce your priorities and dismantle the saboteurs to allow you to be as ambitious as you set out to be.

3. **How can I stay flexible in my plan while remaining committed to my overall vision?**

By now you have a good understanding of your overall vision, and the exercise is meant as a new perspective to validate which parts of your vision you currently are firm on, and which you will (re)consider as you go.

This exercise is also an opportunity to put words on what fears and hesitations will hold you back from seeing opportunity as well as trying to make you give up on your vision.

Key Takeaways: Your Career Blueprint

- **Blueprints turn insights into action.** Combine the Three Dimensions into a strategic, adaptable plan for your career.
- **Goals provide focus.** Define actionable objectives that align with your values, aspirations, and growth areas.
- **Balance is key.** Prioritize different dimensions based on your current stage, ensuring flexibility as your career evolves.

Coach's Corner

When coaching on the Blueprint my focus is to help you identify the actions that will take you towards your goals, and help you avoid time sinks that you will eventually give up on because they are not right for you. A key step of that is having the priorities right so you know what to let go if needed.

An additional question to go deeper on priorities could be:

"If you had to achieve your career goals in half the time you planned, what would you focus on and what would you let go of?"

CHAPTER 11

MANAGING TRANSITIONS

Career transitions are inevitable, whether they're planned or unexpected. At this point in the process, you've laid the groundwork with a clear vision, identified your strengths, and built a framework for your next steps. Now it's time to address the mindset and adaptability needed to navigate career changes successfully.

This chapter focuses on embracing transitions with confidence, staying adaptable, and recognizing the importance of visibility. Keeping your LinkedIn and resume updated allows you to showcase your evolving achievements and remain open to opportunities.

Transitions as Opportunities

Transitions, whether big or small, can feel intimidating. However, they are also opportunities to grow, align more closely with your values, and step into new potential.

The key is shifting your perspective: instead of fearing the unknown, view it as a chance to explore what's possible.

Types of Transitions

- **Voluntary Transitions:** When you're ready for a new role, industry, or challenge.
- **Involuntary Transitions:** When circumstances force change, such as layoffs or organizational shifts.
- **Growth-Driven Transitions:** Natural evolutions in your career as your skills, goals, or aspirations change.

Questions to Consider During a Transition

- What excites you about this potential change?
- What challenges might arise, and how can you prepare for them?
- How does this transition align with your vision and values?

The Mindset of Adaptability

Adaptability is a cornerstone of career success, especially during transitions. Being adaptable doesn't mean abandoning your plans; it means being flexible enough to adjust them without losing sight of your overall goals.

Adaptability is one of the key skills that will both differentiate you from others and will ensure that your plan stays relevant to you. One thing to keep in mind is that every time you learn new skills or gain new experiences - you change! Being adaptable is a key part of your own Pivotal Edge.

Having a mindset of adaptability is also something that people around you will benefit from just by your example. And you will find that some negotiations will be easier when grounded in this mindset.

Adopting a Growth Mindset

- View setbacks as learning opportunities rather than failures.
- Stay curious and open to new experiences, even when they push you out of your comfort zone.

Building Resilience

- Be clear on your purpose. It will help you to see perspective in challenging situations.
- Focus on what you can control, such as your attitude and actions.
- Create routines that provide stability during periods of uncertainty and utilize your social support whether it is guidance, emotional support or just someone who listens.
- Seeing challenges as opportunities for growth is a key part to maintaining optimism and positive thinking which again is crucial to resilience.
- Practice your problem solving skills. Resilient individuals are generally good at breaking down complex issues into parts that are easier to manage and solve.
- Exercise self-compassion. Be kind to yourself, also when things do not go as you planned. Remember, failure is not final, it's feedback.

Visibility During Transitions

As you navigate career changes, staying visible to your network will help you stay on their radar for future opportunities.

The most efficient way to keep your professional network in your loop is by regularly updating your LinkedIn profile and your resume with your latest achievements. Doing this will up the chance of you getting interesting opportunities.

Keeping 1:1 contact with some of your contacts is also a good way to stay on the radar – find a cadence that makes sense both ways and I recommend the approach of a giving mindset without expectation of reciprocation.

Why Visibility Matters:

- It helps others see the value you bring to new roles or projects.
- It signals that you are active, adaptable, and continuously growing.

Quick Tips for Updates:

- Highlight recent accomplishments, particularly those that align with your future vision.
- Use your LinkedIn profile summary to share your evolving professional goals.
- Keep language action-oriented and focused on impact.

Chapter Exercises

Transition Mapping

- Identify a potential or current career transition. Outline the opportunities it presents, challenges to address, and steps you can take to navigate it confidently.

Visibility Audit

- Review your LinkedIn profile and resume. What needs updating to reflect your current journey? Highlight at least one achievement or new skill that aligns with your vision.

Key Takeaways

- Transitions are opportunities to grow, align with your values, and explore new directions.
- A mindset of adaptability and resilience will help you navigate the unknown with confidence.
- Keeping your LinkedIn and resume updated ensures your visibility and positions you for new opportunities.

Coach's Corner

When coaching you around transitions my main focus is to help you explore your mindset of adaptability in combination with your growth mindset. Many things will be outside your control, and will present opportunity when you do not try to control every detail, and being adaptable where you do not see negative impact to your overall plan can open doors you didn't plan for.

An additional question to build perspective could be:

"What's one opportunity you've ignored or dismissed during a transition, and how might revisiting it open new doors?"

CHAPTER 12

SUSTAINING GROWTH AND LEARNING

Reaching your career goals will be an achievement worth celebrating - but it's not the end of your journey. Sustaining growth and continuous learning are key to long-term career fulfillment.

This chapter ties together the insights and strategies from the book, showing how to maintain momentum, adapt to new challenges, and build habits that support ongoing personal and professional development.

This chapter also serves as a motivational reflection, emphasizing the lasting value of aligning your career with your values and aspirations.

While some of it will already be familiar to you from the other chapters I have compiled it in context in this chapter to give you a quick perspective on what it takes to sustain your growth and learning.

The Long-Term Benefits of the Framework

The framework you've worked through in this book isn't a one-time solution - it's a tool you can revisit and adapt as your career evolves. By periodically reassessing your values, strengths, and aspirations, you can ensure your career remains aligned with your authentic self.

Key Benefits of Alignment

- **Clarity:** Knowing what you want helps you make confident decisions.
- **Satisfaction:** Aligning your work with your values brings deeper fulfillment.
- **Adaptability:** Regular reflection prepares you to navigate change with ease.

Revisiting and Realigning Goals

Career goals aren't static - they grow and evolve just like you. Revisiting your goals periodically ensures they remain relevant and reflective of where you are in life. In the beginning I recommend more frequent revisits, like every three months, and every time you revisit you schedule your next revisit in your calendar based on what actions etc. you have for the coming period.

What should trigger a reassessment?

- After major life or career changes (e.g., promotions, family milestones).
- At regular intervals (e.g., annually or every 18 months).
- When you feel a sense of stagnation or misalignment.

Questions to Ask During Reassessment:

- What's working well in my career right now?
- Where do I feel limited, and what's causing that feeling?

- Are my current goals still aligned with my values and aspirations?

Strategies for Lifelong Growth

Growth isn't about constant change—it's about staying curious and open to new opportunities for learning and self-improvement.

Building Habits for Continuous Learning:

- Dedicate time to professional development, such as attending workshops, earning certifications, or taking online courses.
- Stay informed about industry trends to remain relevant and adaptable.
- Cultivate a mindset of curiosity—ask questions, seek feedback, and explore new areas of interest.

Leveraging Support Systems:

- Engage with mentors or peer groups to share insights and stay motivated.
- Join professional communities or networks that encourage learning and collaboration.
- Reflect with accountability partners who can help you track your progress.

Chapter Exercises

1. **Your Growth Map:**

   Outline 3-5 skills, experiences, or areas of knowledge you want to develop over the next year. For each, note one action step to start working toward it.

2. **Re-energize an Area of Stagnation:**

   Identify one area of your career that feels stagnant or underutilized. Brainstorm three ways to bring fresh energy to that area, whether by learning something new, seeking out a mentor, or shifting your approach.

Key Takeaways

- Sustaining growth means continuously aligning your career with your evolving self.
- Regular reassessment helps you stay adaptable and maintain clarity in your direction.
- Lifelong learning, curiosity, and supportive relationships are the cornerstones of lasting career fulfillment.
- Momentum builds success. Consistent small actions over time lead to significant, sustainable growth.

Coach's Corner

When coaching you around sustaining personal growth my focus is to help you explore different perspectives to ensure that you feel that you can make informed decisions instead of making assumptions which can limit your opportunities.

An additional question to build perspective could be:

"If you could no longer rely on your current strengths, what entirely new skill or area of expertise would you develop to future-proof your career?"

CHAPTER 13

BUILDING YOUR CAREER PLAN

Turning Insight into Action

Throughout this book, you've explored your values, strengths, and aspirations, clarified what you want and don't want in your career, and worked on overcoming obstacles. Now, it's time to bring it all together into a structured career plan - your roadmap to success.

A career plan is not just a document; it's a dynamic tool that helps you stay focused, measure progress, and adapt to changes along the way. Whether you're aiming for a complete career transformation or fine-tuning your current path, your plan will serve as your guide.

What to Include in Your Career Plan

To create an actionable career plan, make sure it contains the following key elements:

1. Vision Summary

A clear, concise summary of your career vision. What does success look like to you? Include the key components you aim to achieve and how they align with your values.

Example:
"In three years, I want to transition into a leadership role in a purpose-driven organization, using my skills in strategy and team building to make a meaningful impact."

2. Timeline

Break your journey into manageable phases. Highlight key dates or periods to track your progress.

Example:

- *Phase 1: Building foundational skills (6 months)*
- *Phase 2: Expanding my network and exploring opportunities (12 months)*
- *Phase 3: Transitioning into my desired role (18-24 months)*

3. Milestones

Define major achievements that will mark progress toward your vision. These should be tangible and motivating.

Example:

- *"Complete advanced Communication certification by Month 6."*
- *"Attend three industry events and meet five new connections by Month 12."*

4. Action List

This is your task list. Each action should include:

- Action Name
- Description
- Target Date
- Priority
- Status (*Defined, Ongoing, Paused, Completed*)
- Dependency (*What needs to happen first?*)

- Support Network (*Who can help?*)
- Notes

Example Action:

- **Action Name:** Attend leadership workshop
- **Description:** Enroll in a 2-day leadership development program to enhance team-building skills.
- **Target Date:** March 15th
- **Priority:** High
- **Status:** Defined
- **Dependency:** Approval from employer for funding
- **Who Can Help:** HR manager
- **Notes:** Check for early-bird discounts.

5. Skills Development Plan

Outline the skills you need to build or enhance, along with a plan for how to develop them. Include timelines and resources such as courses, mentors, or hands-on projects.

Example:

- **Skill:** Public speaking
- **Current Proficiency:** 3/5
- **Relevance to Goals:** High
- **Action Plan:** Enroll in Toastmasters and practice presentations monthly.

6. Networking Map

Identify key people and communities that can support your journey. Include specific actions to strengthen these connections.

Example:

- Reach out to former colleagues on LinkedIn to explore potential opportunities.
- Join a professional association related to your industry.
- Schedule monthly coffee chats with mentors or peers.

7. Obstacles and Solutions

Anticipate challenges and prepare strategies to address them.

Example:

- **Obstacle:** Lack of experience in strategic planning.
- **Solution:** Volunteer for cross-functional projects to gain exposure.

8. Metrics for Success

Decide how you will measure your progress and success. Metrics can include role changes, certifications, increased responsibilities, or personal growth.

Example:

- *"Secure a leadership role by Year 3."*
- *"Complete two certifications within 18 months."*

9. Reflection Log and Review Schedule

Plan to revisit and revise your career plan regularly. Reflect on what's working, what's not, and adjust as needed.

Example:

- Schedule quarterly reviews of your plan.
- Note lessons learned and update goals accordingly.

Coach's Corner

When coaching you around building your career plan my focus is empowering your decisions, enabling you to be ambitious in your goals and the actions to implement them.

A successful plan is one that will take you outside your comfort zone, challenge your thinking, and still have a realistic chance of success.

An additional question to give perspective on your plan:

"What would your career plan look like if you removed all perceived constraints, including time, money, or other people's expectations?"

CHAPTER 14

CONCLUSIONS

Embracing the Journey

Throughout this book, you've explored the essential elements that shape your career: your strengths, values, boundaries, goals, and purpose. By reflecting on these in the perspective of the Dimensions, you've given yourself the gift of perspective - a chance to see your career with fresh eyes, challenge old assumptions, and reconnect with what truly matters.

This journey is about more than building a career; it's about creating a professional life that reflects who you are, what you believe in, and the impact you wish to have. Your career isn't just a path; it's a reflection of your evolving self and the choices you make along the way.

Your Career Plan: A Living Compass

The career plan you've created isn't set in stone. It's a living document that evolves as you grow and learn. Your priorities may shift, new opportunities will arise, and unexpected challenges may come your way. But with your plan in hand, you are equipped to navigate these changes with clarity and confidence.

Start by drafting your vision, identifying your milestones, and taking those first steps. Remember, progress is rarely linear, and obstacles are inevitable. But each step you take brings you closer to a career that aligns with your purpose, values, and strengths.

Let your plan act as your compass - a tool that keeps you grounded and focused, even as the world around you change. It's your guide to navigating challenges, seizing opportunities, and building a career that feels genuinely, powerfully yours.

The Value of Ongoing Self-Assessment

Self-reflection doesn't end with the final page of this book; it's a lifelong practice. As you grow and circumstances shift, return to the exercises and insights you've gained here. Revisit your strengths, reassess your values, and check in with your evolving purpose. Adapt your goals, boundaries, and aspirations to reflect where you are today and where you want to go.

This flexibility will keep your career vibrant and fulfilling, allowing you to stay true to yourself no matter where your path leads. Periodically revisit your career blueprint to refine your goals, realign your direction, and build on the foundation you've created.

Moving Forward with Confidence and Purpose

A meaningful career is built on both purpose and adaptability. By staying connected to the Core of You, the Core of Challenge, and the Core of Purpose, you are equipped to make choices that reflect your authentic self and evolving aspirations.

Your future begins with the steps you take today. Embrace

change, pursue growth, and allow your career to reflect the best version of you. Let your plan be your pivotal edge, capturing everything you've worked toward and serving as a reminder of your incredible potential.

A Final Wish

Thank you for taking on this journey of self-discovery and career transformation with me.

I hope this book has delivered to its promise for you and that you have picked up new insights about yourself!?

My wish for you is that your onward journey will be both fulfilling and impactful, and that you will stay in control - leading a career that feels genuinely, powerfully yours.

May your journey take you to new places!

Kindly,

Henning Bech
Your Coach

APPENDIX A

FREQUENTLY ASKED QUESTIONS

My Career Plan

Here are some of the questions I frequently get from clients

- **What details should be in my plan?**

You need the details required for you to follow your plan, and from my experience most people benefit from having what is in Chapter 13

  - If you want to keep it simpler then I suggest that you use it all but start with less detail on most except for the actions.
  - The key element is the Action List, but having the other parts described will help you with motivation and adapting to changes and communicating your vision.

- **What format do you recommend for my plan?**

It's important that you use the tools that support you the best, for some that is having the plan in a paper planner, for me I prefer digital tools that I can access from my laptop, phone and my 'digital paper' notebook.

I keep my own plan in a spreadsheet as it supports how I do action tracking. Some of my clients use digital tools that support dragging cards through a flow.

Key message is do it in any way that you will consistently use else you lose traction and often sight of your goals and vision as well.

- **How often should I revisit this career framework?**

That depends on how much activity you have on your actions. Some periods will be more active than others as making changes to your career often requires time to learn new skills, build more experiences etc.

I recommend consulting your plan and your journal at least every three months the first year to make sure that it is still relevant and up-to-date, and you are in sync with what's ahead of you. Then revisit when new opportunities present themselves to reflect on how they affect your overall plan.

- **What if I change my mind a few months down the road and feel that I need a new vision?**

First, I would recommend that you reflect on what has changed for you.

Is it new opportunities that have challenged your perspective? Is it fears? Or something entirely different? Whatever it is, first you need to understand why it did not surface while you went through the process of this book.

If it shows that you really do need to define a new vision then just start over and follow the process, and it could even be beneficial for you to consult a coach to work through it and help you crystallize your thinking.

The Things Not Covered by the Book

- **Why is the book not covering more of the coaching behind the framework?**

The intention with this book is not to educate coaches, but to enable you to take control of your own career based on a solid foundation of personal insight.

I have included “Coach’s Corner” and “A Note from Your Coach” where I think it can add value to your journey by giving you a taste of what I do and hope it can serve as inspiration for further reflection.

- **How do I get A4 PDF with the detailed visual representation of the framework?**

To keep the size of the book practical for different types of reading styles the A4 sized framework visuals can be downloaded from my website https://pivotaledge.me for free alongside other free resources when you register your purchase of this book with your email address.

APPENDIX B

EXAMPLES FOR SELECT CHAPTERS

Chapter 2: Your Strengths

These examples are not to replace your own reflection and work, and only serve as contextual inspiration if you haven't reflected on this area before.

Natural Strengths	Learned Skills	Current Utilization	Future Development
Empathy	Advanced negotiation skills	Building team morale	Learning to navigate high-stakes negotiations
Strategic thinking	Public speaking	Creating project roadmaps	Developing storytelling for impactful presentations
Conflict resolution	Data analysis	Managing team dynamics	Using data to predict potential conflicts
Adaptability	Budget planning	Handling last-minute changes	Mastering long-term financial forecasting

Chapter 3: Your Values

These examples are not to replace your own reflection and work, and only serve as contextual inspiration if you haven't reflected on this area before.

Value	Importance (1-5)	How It Shows In My Career	How I Want to Honor It Moving Forward
Integrity	5	Ensuring honest communication	Prioritizing transparent leadership
Creativity	4	Developing innovative solutions	Allocating time for brainstorming
Work-life balance	3	Encouraging flexible schedules	Setting clear boundaries with clients
Team collaboration	5	Building inclusive work environments	Fostering cross-department partnerships

Chapter 4: What You Want to Work With

These examples are not to replace your own reflection and work, and only serve as contextual inspiration if you haven't reflected on this area before.

Skill	Current Proficiency (1-5)	Relevance to Future Goals	Action Plan for Development
Leadership Coaching	4	High	Complete advanced coaching certification
Digital marketing	2	Medium	Take online courses on social media ads
Process optimization	3	High	Learn Lean Six Sigma methodologies
Emotional intelligence	5	High	Attend workshops to deepen interpersonal skills

Chapter 8: The Three Dimensions

These examples are not to replace your own reflection and work, and only serve as contextual inspiration if you haven't reflected on this area before.

Dimension	Key Elements
Core of You	Empathy, adaptability
Core of Challenge	Strategic thinking, leadership
Core of Purpose	Integrity, work-life balance

Chapter 10: Building Your Career Blueprint

These examples are not to replace your own reflection and work, and only serve as contextual inspiration if you haven't reflected on this area before.

Dimension	Goal	Timeline	Key Actions	Dependencies
Core of You	Deepen emotional intelligence	3 months	Attend a workshop	Workshop availability
Core of Challenge	Expand leadership influence	6 months	Take on a cross-functional project	Approval from leadership
Core of Purpose	Align role with values	1 year	Explore new job opportunities	Networking opportunities

Chapter 11: Managing Transitions

These examples are not to replace your own reflection and work, and only serve as contextual inspiration if you haven't reflected on this area before.

Type of Transition	Opportunities	Challenges	Key Actions for Adaption
Role Change	New responsibilities	Learning new skills	Set up a mentor relationship
Industry Shift	Broadening expertise	Adjusting to new workplace culture	Research industry trends
Geographic Relocation	Expanding global networks	Adapting to a new environment	Join local professional groups

What's Next for You?

You Are the Key to Your Career's Next Chapter

Every decision you've made to this point has brought you here - reading this book, reflecting on your strengths, values, purpose and more. And now, the next chapter of your career isn't just waiting to be written; it's waiting to be lived.

Think about this: *Your career is not defined by past roles, titles, or even setbacks. It's shaped by the choices you make moving forward.*

The work you've done through this book isn't just an exercise; it's a declaration that your career deserves intention, growth, and fulfillment.

Yes, obstacles will come. Yes, doubts may creep in. But with the clarity you've gained, you're equipped to face those moments with confidence. The path won't always be straight or predictable, but it's yours - and that's what makes it powerful and what I call Your Pivotal Edge.

Take a moment to breathe in this truth:

You are not stuck. You are not limited. You are capable.

And as you continue, remember this: *Your career is YOUR story.* ***Own it, grow it, love it*** *and don't be afraid to make it extraordinary.*

Join The Movement

Your journey doesn't end here; it's just beginning. To help you keep the momentum going, I've created a set of free resources designed to support you on your path. These and more to come will be available via my book site and include:

- **Reflection Exercises**: Simple exercises to help you keep focus as you execute on your blueprint plan.
- **Career Planning Tool**: Template for mapping out milestones, goals, and action steps.
- **Exclusive Insights**: Monthly emails with practical tips, strategies, and inspiring stories from others on similar journeys.

Joining is simple and completely free. Visit https://pivotaledge.me to sign up and gain access to these tools.

Why sign up? Because the journey of building a fulfilling career is better with support. This isn't just about checking boxes - it's about creating a life that feels aligned, purpose-driven, and uniquely yours.

Let's keep the conversation going. Your career transformation doesn't stop with this book - it grows with every step you take from here.

Copyrights and Used Resources

Printed in Great Britain
by Amazon

57878054R10066